THE **INTERNET SAFETY COLORING & ACTIVITY BOOK**

with Olivia and Friends!

Nathan LaChine &
Karina StarkHart

Illustrated by Annabelle Betts

I0529214

For permissions, inquiries, or additional information, please contact:

EvergreenCaregiverSupport.org

Self-published by

Evergreen Caregiver Support

Lakewood, WA, USA

ISBN: 979-8-9928534-3-8

Cover Design and Illustrations by Annabelle Betts

Co-Author Karina StarkHart, MA, LMHCA

Printed in the United States of America

☆ OLIVIA ♡

Internet Vocab Word Search

```
J T R O L L D U E M E M M U Y B Z C X
R Q L Z Y G Q W T S E I R A D N U O B
I X Z M O N O U K S R U D Q H C C I P
V G O G G I R V O C K H L O C G Y R T
B N D D R F X V L O G K Z C A A I G N
K I Q T O O Y W V G N O W S C V N V E
W Y O C O O I D P P A Q M Y A P P W S
L L I O M P J R J D B O N C G X E N N
Q L D Q I S S C R D Z T Y T P T R B O
J U Y Y N C C B I J B S G G Z T S N C
F B N C G O M F X K X X P I K M O Z N
M R G N I T X E T J T P W W N U N E I
H E B X X I Z I U B R A C A O R A K K
Z B J J C U U Y K O L C Y X X X L S M
I Y F D C M P S F P E S K U K D M Y S
V C X G Z N F I K R A I L O M M D I Q
G I K I Q Z L I F T U O H S U T E F B
Z Z R Q U E K O Q E A S F M Z Q A F S
J C G U F N E R U V V T O J H U P I Z
D R O W S S A P S E I K O O C M I E O
```

Word Bank

1. vlog
2. spoofing
3. boundaries
4. cookies
5. app
6. profile
7. privacy
8. grooming
9. texting
10. troll
11. personal
12. consent
13. virus
14. password
15. cyberbullying
16. meme

Match each text to one of Olivia's friends, use their profiles as clues!
Cross out texts that don't seem like they are from real people.

@paipixiep
Paisley (she/her)

Junior karate orange belt!!!
Usually gaming with @o.live.laugh.<3
or pressing cool leaves :o

@alex.the.asteroid
Alex (he/him)

spaced out again...
fav comic right now: 2 many to list

@leon.lion
Leo (he/him)

Esp + Eng
Vote Leo for junior theatre club pres
played the lion in Wizard of Oz last year

@liamgaming2
Liam (he/him)

biggest introvert
i draw sometimes :P

This is Karl from [COMPANY] your package was delayed due to missing profile info. Click here to learn more. e493tfne5yyh.com

Alex sent me this meme thought you might like it 2 :P

Hope your summer has been good Ive been at drama camp!!

Hey olivia can't play our game until later, i have karate practice. ttyl :)

CLICK HERE TO CLAIM REWARD ewi943hfr.com

Liam said you have book 3 of Cat Astronauts, can I borrow it?

You can delete and report messages as junk or spam if they are from someone you don't know.

I like to check with my friends in-person to make sure a profile or number is really them.

Spot the difference!

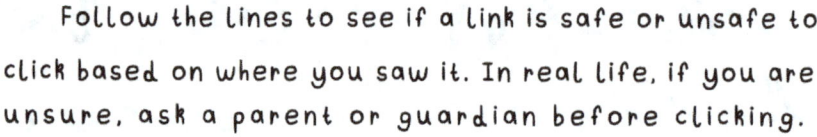
Safe or Unsafe Links

Follow the lines to see if a link is safe or unsafe to click based on where you saw it. In real life, if you are unsure, ask a parent or guardian before clicking.

Link from:

Mom

Best friend you've messaged a lot before

A friend you've never got a message from before

Text from a number you don't recognize

Message from an account you don't recognize

Official account of your school

Might not really be them!

Dots + Boxes!

How to play: Take turns connecting one dot to another. If a box is made, whoever makes the closing line puts their initial inside the box. The person with the most boxes at the end wins!

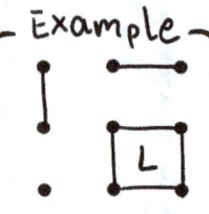

 ## Creating Secure Passwords

Cross out the password options that would be easy to guess, color in the most secure ones.

alex1234

maxthedog

~Asteroid51%!

password

oMg1t'$0liviA8

@c0ol*Band776

abcd

liamjones

What makes a password secure (hard to guess)? Check the answer key for which password examples were best. Try coming up with your own below!

_____

_____

_____

_____

_____

_____

Color by number

1- white   2- blue   3- yellow   4- pink   5-black

3	3	3	3	3	3	3	3	3	3	3	3	3	3	3	3	3	3	3	3	3	3	3	3
3	3	3	3	3	3	3	3	3	3	3	3	3	3	3	3	3	3	3	3	3	3	3	3
3	3	3	3	3	5	5	3	3	3	3	3	3	3	3	3	3	3	3	2	2	2	2	2
3	3	3	3	3	5	4	5	5	3	3	3	3	3	2	2	2	2	2	2	2	2	2	2
3	3	3	3	3	5	4	4	5	3	3	3	2	2	2	2	2	2	1	2	2	2	2	2
3	3	3	3	5	5	4	4	5	3	2	2	2	2	1	2	2	1	1	1	2	2	2	2
3	3	3	3	5	4	4	4	5	2	2	2	2	2	1	1	5	4	1	1	2	2	2	2
3	3	3	3	5	4	4	4	5	2	2	2	2	1	1	5	4	4	1	1	2	2	2	2
3	3	3	5	5	4	4	4	5	2	2	2	2	1	1	5	4	4	4	1	2	2	2	2
3	3	3	5	5	5	4	5	5	5	5	1	1	1	5	4	4	4	4	1	2	2	2	2
3	3	3	3	5	5	5	5	5	5	1	1	1	1	4	4	4	4	1	2	2	2	2	2
3	3	3	3	3	5	5	5	5	5	1	1	1	1	1	4	5	1	1	2	2	2	2	2
3	3	3	3	5	1	5	5	5	5	1	1	5	1	1	1	5	1	1	2	2	2	2	2
3	3	3	2	5	5	5	5	1	1	1	1	1	5	1	1	1	1	2	2	2	2	2	2
3	3	2	2	5	5	1	1	1	1	1	5	5	1	1	5	2	2	2	2	2	2	2	2
3	3	2	5	5	1	5	5	5	1	1	5	5	1	1	5	1	5	5	5	2	2	2	2
3	3	2	5	1	1	5	5	5	1	1	1	1	1	1	5	1	5	5	5	5	5	5	5
3	2	2	5	1	1	1	1	1	1	1	1	1	1	1	5	1	1	5	5	5	5	5	5
3	2	2	5	5	4	4	5	1	1	5	1	1	5	1	1	1	1	1	1	5	5	5	5
3	2	2	2	5	1	4	4	1	5	1	5	1	5	1	1	1	1	1	1	1	1	1	5
2	2	2	2	2	5	1	1	1	1	1	5	5	1	1	1	1	1	1	1	1	1	1	5
2	2	2	2	2	2	5	1	1	1	5	1	1	1	1	1	1	1	1	1	1	1	1	5
2	2	2	2	2	2	2	5	1	1	1	1	1	1	1	1	1	1	1	1	1	1	5	5

LEVEL UP!

Olivia has a research project in science class about grizzly bears, help her find a reliable website based on the url!

(The urls are examples, not real links)

Grizzlyloversforum.com
DEAD END
Anyone can post in a forum, not a reliable source.

CoolBearFacts4kidz.com
DEAD END
Using slang, shortened words, or misspellings can tip you off that a website is not very professional or reliable.

InternationalBearResearch Coalition.org/GrizzlyInfo
Looks reliable!
.org is used by non-profit or educational organizations often with verified information and research.

# # #

HDR

SLO-MO   VIDEO   PHOTO   SQUARE   PANO

What Would Your Mood Look Like as an Emoji?

Draw three custom emojis that show how you feel in different situations.

When you're proud of yourself

When you're overwhelmed

When you're super hyped

Cross out the fake account, look for missing information, stolen identities and photos, and if they have reasonable amounts of followers and following.

O.live.laugh<3   Private account 20 followers 30 following
Olivia (she/her)
i <3 gaming and cute bears!

AL.angelx   Private account 31 followers 40 following
Angel (they/them)
🥎 ⚽ omw to championships!
bestie-> @Alextheasteroid

liamgaming2   Private account 18 followers 20 following
Liam (he/him)
🎮 ✏️ biggest introvert. i draw sometimes :P

Al_angelx   Public account 0 followers 402 following
angel

I Spy!

Count how many of each you can find!

☆ __ 🔍 __ 🔎 __ ➹ __ 😃 __ ♡ __ 📶 __

😜 __ 📞 __ 👍 __ ♪ __ 😮 __ 😎 __ ↻ __

HANGOUT

HOLD OFF on meeting anyone you only know online.

ALWAYS talk to a trusted adult first.

NEVER share your location or personal info.

GO with your gut- if something feels weird, it probably is.

ONLY meet up with real-life friends.

USE privacy settings to stay safe.

TELL someone right away if you feel uncomfortable.

Olivia <3

liam

Alex!!!!

angel B)

Internet Vocab Crossword

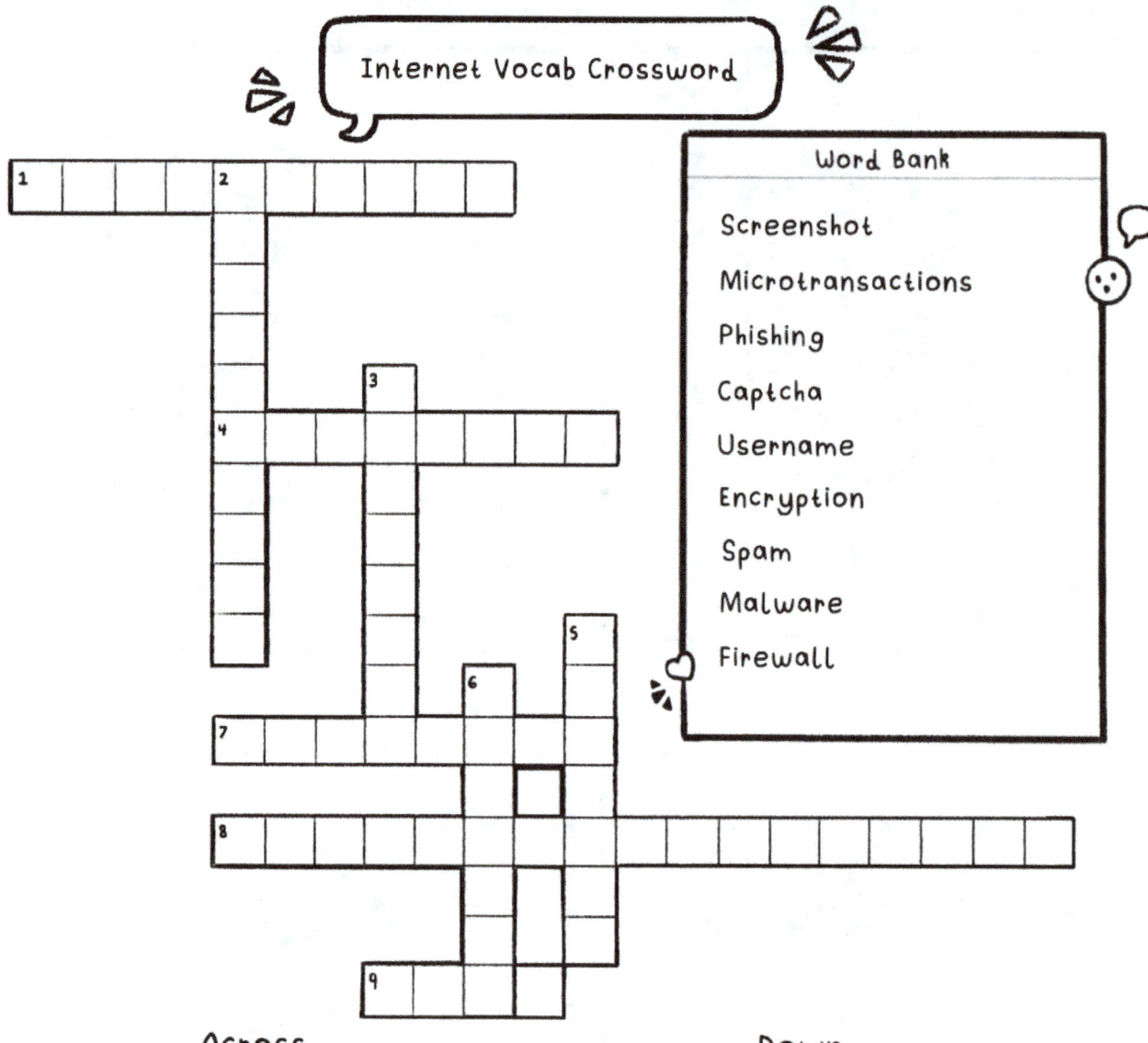

Word Bank

- Screenshot
- Microtransactions
- Phishing
- Captcha
- Username
- Encryption
- Spam
- Malware
- Firewall

Across

1. When content on screen is saved as a picture.

4. A trick where someone pretends to be a trustworthy person to get your personal info, like passwords.

7. Software that helps protect your device from viruses and hackers.

8. Small purchases made within a game or other app, usually with real money, to buy virtual items or unlock special features.

9. Unwanted or junk emails or messages, often from strangers or companies.

Down

2. A process of turning data into a secret code to protect it, ensuring only the intended recipient can read or use it.

3. A name you choose to represent yourself online, like a nickname.

5. Harmful software that can damage your device or steal your information.

6. A security test on websites to make sure you're a real person, not a bot. It usually asks you to type characters or click on certain images.

Cyberbullying Role Play

Someone has been sending Olivia mean messages in her favorite online game for a couple days. They won't leave her alone and she doesn't know what to do.

you mess up every round wtf is your problem

stupidest idiot ive ever seen

tired of seeing you loser noob in my game

you play so bad you must be U G L Y

delete your account already >:(

Circle everything you would do, cross out options that don't sound smart or safe.

Block their account

Report their account

Reply to them with mean messages of your own

Stop playing your favorite game to avoid them

Tell a parent or guardian

Reply apologizing and saying they're right

Is there anything else you would do?

_____

_____

_____

I don't need to post this moment, it can be just for me.

Screen Time Balance

What are some of your favorite offline activities and ways to unplug?

_____

_____

_____

_____

_____

_____

Draw your #1 here!

RMAUSENE _____

WDSSRADPO _____

YBLLIBCERYUNG _____

GVLO _____

PALERSON _____

URIVS _____

EMME _____

IRPYACV _____

SCENTON _____

Decode the Message!

KEY:

A	B	C	D	E	F	G	H	I
☆	🔍	💬	👎	➤	😀	◆	♥	📶

J	K	L	M	N	O	P	Q	R
😛	📞	👍	🎵	😮	★	📷	😎	↻

S	T	U	V	W	X	Y	Z
✉	◆	♡	😊	⚙	🔋	▶	😍

A L W A Y S

T H I N K

S A F E T Y

F I R S T

Resources

Evergreen Caregiver Support
evergreencaregiversupport.org

ECPAT
ecpat.org/bill-of-rights

Interland
beinternetawesome.withgoogle.com/en-us/interland

Interpol
interpol.int/en/Crimes/Crimes-against-children

National Center for Missing and Exploited Youth (NCMEC)
missingkids.org

NetSmartz
netsmartzkids.org

Take it Down
takeitdown.ncmec.org

Thorn
thorn.org

Crisis Text Line
text "HOME" to 741741

The Trevor Project
thetrevorproject.org

988 Lifeline
988lifeline.org

About the Creators

Nathan LaChine is a third generation foster parent and internet safety expert with over 20 years of experience supporting vulnerable youth through therapeutic care and community advocacy. As the founder of Evergreen Caregiver Support, he develops training material, facilitates workshops, and speaks internationally on topics related to youth safety and support for LGBTQIA+ youth. Nathan also advises nonprofit youth advocacy groups, caregivers, and policymakers across his state.

Check out Nathan's trainings, additional information, and resources at EvergreenCaregiverSupport.com.

Karina StarkHart is a mental health therapist with a passion for fostering healthy relationships and personal empowerment. Her background includes more than a decade of social work and education centering youth and parenting support, particularly around topics such as behavior, trauma, and safety.

Connect with her at Desireblooms.com.

Annabelle Betts is an aspiring illustrator who emphasizes visual storytelling for positive impact through illustration, collage, and comics.

Check out Annabelle's comics on Tapas @BananaBelle, illustrations and other projects on Instagram @bananabelleart, and art shop on Etsy, at bananabelleart.etsy.com.

Check out the first Olivia and Friends book, the *Internet Safety Workbook for Tweens*!

Answer Keys

Internet Vocab Word Search

Word Bank

1. vlog
2. spoofing
3. boundaries
4. cookies
5. app
6. profile
7. privacy
8. grooming
9. texting
10. troll
11. personal
12. consent
13. virus
14. password
15. cyberbullying
16. meme

Match each text to one of Olivia's friends, use their profiles as clues! Cross out texts that don't seem like they are from real people.

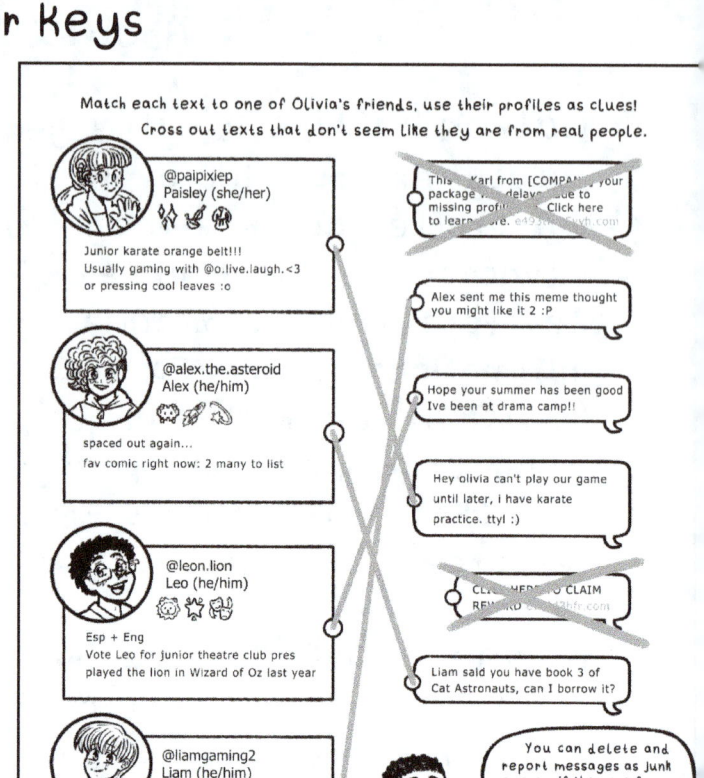

@paipixiep
Paisley (she/her)
Junior karate orange belt!!!
Usually gaming with @o.live.laugh.<3
or pressing cool leaves :o

@alex.the.asteroid
Alex (he/him)
spaced out again...
fav comic right now: 2 many to list

@leon.lion
Leo (he/him)
Esp + Eng
Vote Leo for junior theatre club pres
played the lion in Wizard of Oz last year

@liamgaming2
Liam (he/him)
biggest introvert
i draw sometimes :P

Texts:
- This ~~Karl from [COMPANY] your package will delay due to missing profil... Click here to learn... re. e493...~~
- Alex sent me this meme thought you might like it 2 :P
- Hope your summer has been good Ive been at drama camp!!
- Hey olivia can't play our game until later, i have karate practice. ttyl :)
- ~~CLICK HERE TO CLAIM REWARD...~~
- Liam said you have book 3 of Cat Astronauts, can I borrow it?

Olivia's tips:
- You can delete and report messages as junk or spam if they are from someone you don't know.
- I like to check with my friends in-person to make sure a profile or number is really them.

Spot the difference!

Creating Secure Passwords

Cross out the password options that would be easy to guess, color in the most secure ones.

- ~~alex1234~~
- ~~max...~~
- ~Asteroid51%!
- ~~password~~
- oMg1t'$0liviA8
- @c0ol*Band776
- ~~abcd~~
- ~~liamjones~~

What makes a password secure (hard to guess)? Check the answer key for which password examples were best. Try coming up with your own below!

Answer Keys

Olivia has a research project in science class about grizzly bears, help her find a reliable website based on the url!

(The urls are examples, not real links)

Grizzlyloversforum.com
DEAD END
Anyone can post in a forum, not a reliable source.

CoolBearFacts4kidz.com
DEAD END
Using slang, shortened words, or misspellings can tip you off that a website is not very professional or reliable.

InternationalBearResearch Coalition.org/GrizzlyInfo
Looks reliable!
.org is used by non-profit or educational organizations often with verified information and research.

Match the Shadows!

Odd One Out

Cross out the fake account. Look for missing information, stolen identities and photos, and if they have reasonable amounts of followers and following.

O.live.laugh<3   Private account 20 followers 30 following
Olivia (she/her)
i <3 gaming and cute bears!

AL.angelx   Private account 31 followers 40 following
Angel (they/them)
🌐 ⚽ omw to championships!
bestie-> @Alextheasteroid

liamgaming2   Private account 18 followers 20 following
Liam (he/him)
🎮✏️ biggest introvert. i draw sometimes :P

Al_angelx   Public account 0 followers 49? following
angel

I Spy!

Count how many of each you can find!

☆ 9   🔍 7   💬 7   ➢ 6   😄 6   ♡ 7   📶 5

😛 4   🌙 5   👍 6   🎵 5   😮 4   😎 5   🔄 4

Answer Keys

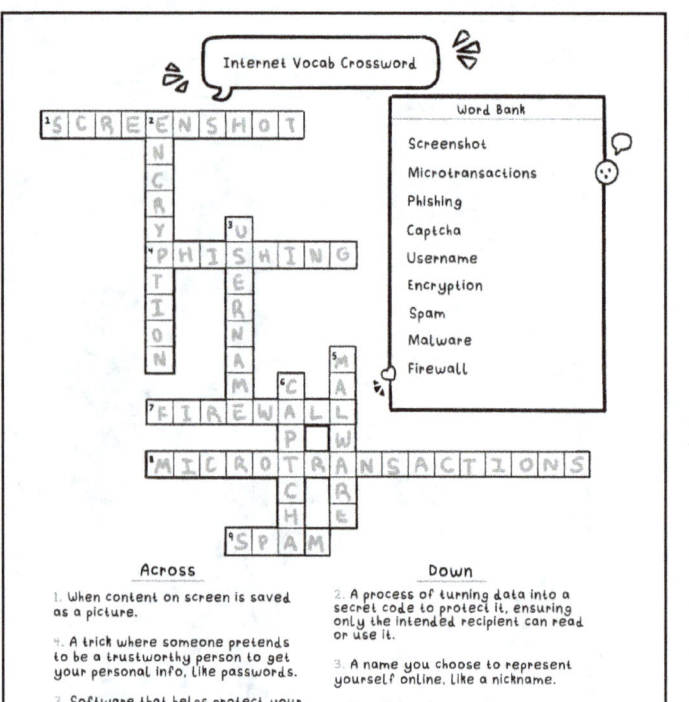

Internet Vocab Crossword

Word Bank:
- Screenshot
- Microtransactions
- Phishing
- Captcha
- Username
- Encryption
- Spam
- Malware
- Firewall

Crossword answers:
- 1 Across: SCREENSHOT
- 2 Down: ENCRYPTION
- 3 Down: USERNAME
- 4 Across: PHISHING
- 5 Down: MALWARE
- 6 Down: CAPTCHE
- 7 Across: FIREWALL
- 8 Across: MICROTRANSACTIONS
- 9 Across: SPAM

Across
1. When content on screen is saved as a picture.

4. A trick where someone pretends to be a trustworthy person to get your personal info, like passwords.

7. Software that helps protect your device from viruses and hackers.

8. Small purchases made within a game or other app, usually with real money, to buy virtual items or unlock special features.

9. Unwanted or junk emails or messages, often from strangers or companies.

Down
2. A process of turning data into a secret code to protect it, ensuring only the intended recipient can read or use it.

3. A name you choose to represent yourself online, like a nickname.

5. Harmful software that can damage your device or steal your information.

6. A security test on websites to make sure you're a real person, not a bot. It usually asks you to type characters or click on certain images.

Cyberbullying Role Play

Someone has been sending Olivia mean messages in her favorite online game for a couple days. They won't leave her alone and she doesn't know what to do.

- you mess up every round wtf is your problem
- stupidest idiot ive ever seen
- tired of seeing you loser noob in my game
- you play so bad you must be U G L Y
- delete your account already >:(

Circle everything you would do, cross out options that don't sound smart or safe.

- Block their account ⭕
- Report their account ⭕
- ~~Reply to them with mean messages of your own~~
- ~~Stop playing your favorite game to avoid them~~
- Tell a parent or guardian ⭕
- ~~Reply apologizing and saying they're right~~

Is there anything else you would do?

_____

_____

_____

Word Unscramble

- RMAUSENE — USERNAME
- WDSSRADPO — PASSWORD
- YBLLIBCERYUNG — CYBERBULLYING
- GVLO — VLOG
- PALERSON — PERSONAL
- URIVS — VIRUS
- EMME — MEME
- IRPYACV — PRIVACY
- SCENTON — CONSENT

Decode the Message!

KEY:

A	B	C	D	E	F	G	H	I
☆	🔍	💬	👎	➤	😃	◇	♥	📶

J	K	L	M	N	O	P	Q	R
😛	📞	👍	🎵	😮	★	📷	😎	↻

S	T	U	V	W	X	Y	Z
✉	◆	♡	😊	⚙	🔋	▷	😍

ALWAYS

THINK

SAFETY

FIRST